On Monday March the twenty-eighth 1188, a great crowd gathered in St David's cathedral to hear the archbishop of Canterbury preach a special sermon. He was on a journey that would take him right round Wales. His guide was ideally suited for the role. He was of a noble Norman family on his father's side, and Welsh on his mother's. He was the cleric, linguist, naturalist, geographer, story-teller, and writer, Gerald of Wales. This book shows something of what Wales was like eight hundred years ago, largely through his eyes. But why was the archbishop of Canterbury preaching in St David's on that March morning?.......

Muslims as well as Christians saw Jerusalem and the surrounding lands as holy places and fought for their possession. These wars were called 'crusades' and had the blessing of the church.

THE LANDS OF A NORMAN

THE PEOPLE

THE LORD HOLDS HIS LAND FROM THE KING | KNIGHTS AND GARRISON | PRIEST | FREEHOLDERS | VILLEINS | SERFS

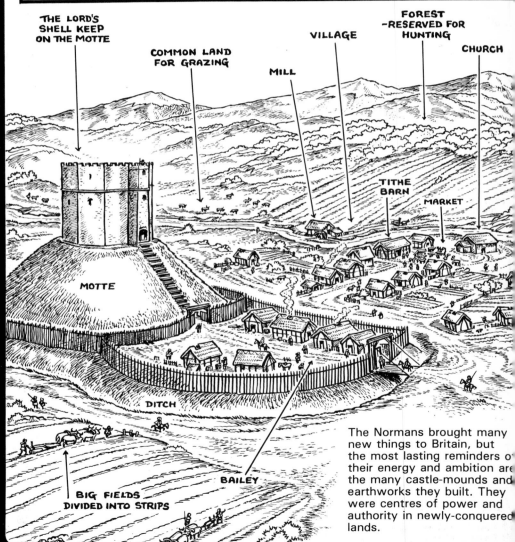

THE LORD'S SHELL KEEP ON THE MOTTE

COMMON LAND FOR GRAZING

MILL

VILLAGE

FOREST –RESERVED FOR HUNTING

CHURCH

TITHE BARN

MARKET

MOTTE

DITCH

BAILEY

BIG FIELDS DIVIDED INTO STRIPS

The Normans brought many new things to Britain, but the most lasting reminders of their energy and ambition are the many castle-mounds and earthworks they built. They were centres of power and authority in newly-conquered lands.

LORD OF THE MARCHES

6

FIGHTING MEN OF THE TIME

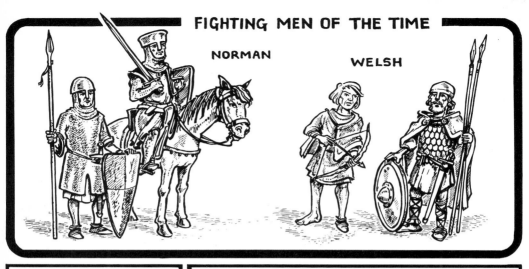

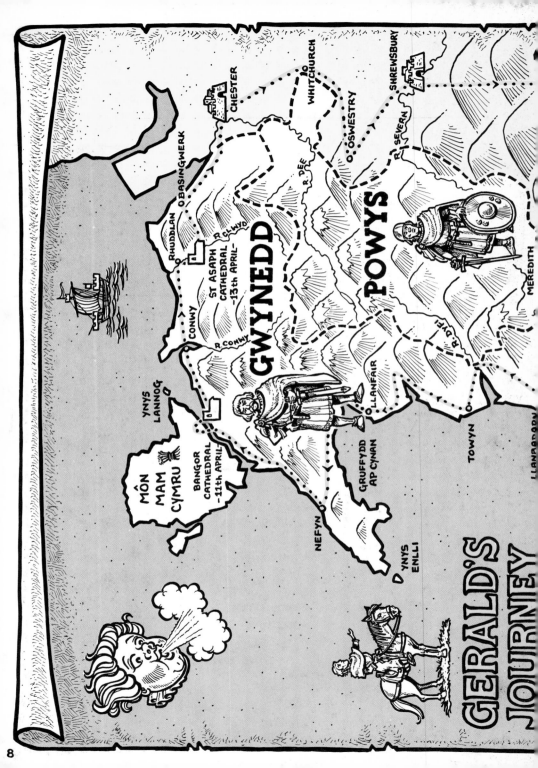

GERALD'S JOURNEY

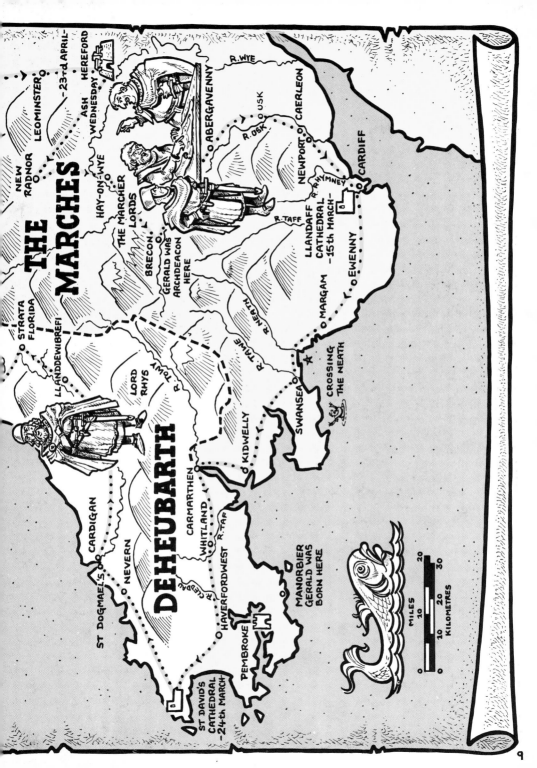

9

Gerald believed that there had once been an archbishop in the city of St David's, not subject to the authority of the archbishop of Canterbury. His secret dream was to see the archbishopric restored, with him in the chair! St David's was a famous place of pilgrimage — two journeys there counted the same as one to Rome.

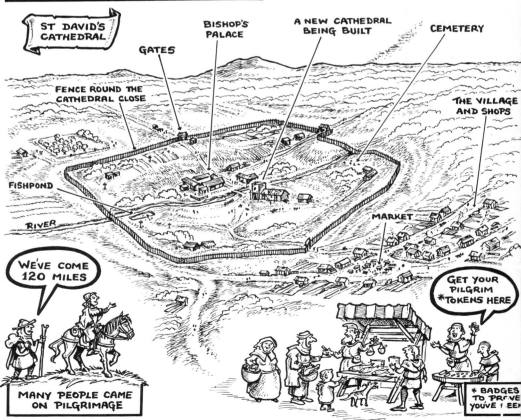

A WEEK'S TRAVELLING AND PREACHING FOUND THE WEARY GROUP AT STRATA FLORIDA

LOOK A BEAVER *

* THEN FOUND IN WALES

WE'LL REST A DAY OR TWO IN THE MONASTERY

IT IS COMFORTING TO KNOW THAT WHEREVER THERE IS A CHURCH THERE IS A PLACE OF WELCOME AND PEACE

THE MONKS WERE VERY GOOD FARMERS

HURDLES

AND SO...

I'LL WRITE MORE TOMORROW

3RD APRIL 1188

NOT EVERYONE IS AS COMFY...

EVEN WITH ALL MY CLOTHES ON I'M STILL COLD!

COMMUNAL BED

HIS FEET STINK

ONE STIFF ROUGH SHEET

HARD MATTRESS STUFFED WITH REEDS

BRECWAST!

OH GOOD.. ..GROATS * THAT'LL BUILD UP MY STRENGTH

* – A COARSE PORRIDGE

"...the mountains are very high, with narrow ridges and a great number of very sharp peaks..."

GWYNEDD!

WE'LL SOON BE IN WALES PROPER

CLEANING TEETH WITH HAZEL-SHOOTS – AND POLISHING WITH A RAG

THE SHEPHERDS CAN CALL TO EACH OTHER ACROSS THE VALLEYS

THE PEOPLE

| Y TYWYSOG (THE PRINCE) | TEULU (FAMILY) | DISTAIN (STEWARD) | OFFEIRIAD (PRIEST) | PENCERDD (CHIEF POET) | YNAD (JUDGE) | FREEMEN | BOND MEN |

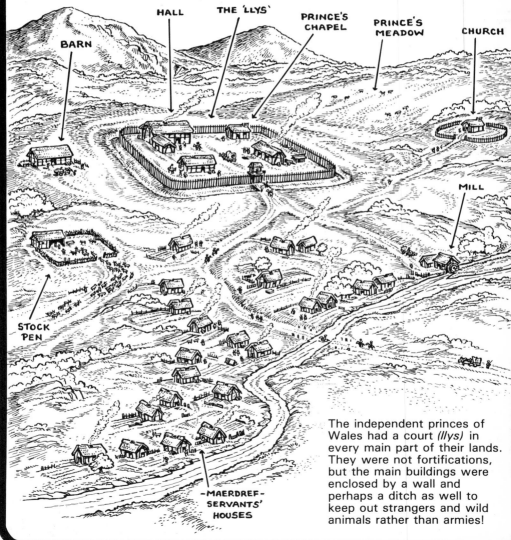

BARN

HALL

THE 'LLYS'

PRINCE'S CHAPEL

PRINCE'S MEADOW

CHURCH

MILL

STOCK PEN

-MAERDREF- SERVANTS' HOUSES

The independent princes of Wales had a court *(llys)* in every main part of their lands. They were not fortifications, but the main buildings were enclosed by a wall and perhaps a ditch as well to keep out strangers and wild animals rather than armies!

PRINCE OF WALES

EVENTUALLY....

THE CHESHIRE PLAIN... NOW WE TURN SOUTH

OSWESTRY 14th APRIL

"...we were entertained most splendidly and sumptuously in the English fashion..."

TIRED WE MAY BE, BUT 3,000 FIGHTING MEN HAVE TAKEN THE CROSS, ALL EXPERIENCED WITH THE SPEAR AND ARROW

ON THE MENU TONIGHT... DUCK, CHICKEN, SALMON, EEL, RABBIT...PASTRIES.. SAUCES..PEPPER..WINE

CIVILISATION AT LAST

HEREFORD

"...we returned once more to the place from which we had begun this journey through Wales..."

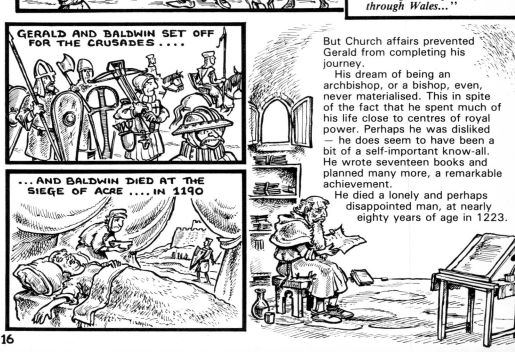

GERALD AND BALDWIN SET OFF FOR THE CRUSADES....

...AND BALDWIN DIED AT THE SIEGE OF ACRE .... IN 1190

But Church affairs prevented Gerald from completing his journey.

His dream of being an archbishop, or a bishop, even, never materialised. This in spite of the fact that he spent much of his life close to centres of royal power. Perhaps he was disliked — he does seem to have been a bit of a self-important know-all. He wrote seventeen books and planned many more, a remarkable achievement.

He died a lonely and perhaps disappointed man, at nearly eighty years of age in 1223.